6.9.77

THE BETHLEHEM TREE
A Family Advent Resource Book

MARY LOUISE TIETJEN

Library of Congress
Catalog Card Number: 76-9364

ISBN: 0-8091-1949-8

Published by Paulist Press
Editorial Office: 1865 Broadway, N.Y., N.Y. 10023
Business Office: 400 Sette Drive, Paramus, N.J. 07652

Printed and bound in the
United States of America

CONTENTS

INTRODUCTION

This is a book for parents and their children, to help them make ready the way of the Lord. It is offered as an Advent resource so that, with a little loving care, Advent can become for us a time of search and discovery, of great expectation and deepened understanding. Families will find here things to talk about, things to read, and things to do—including the making of ten symbolic ornaments for the Christmas tree.

Each of the simply made decorations has something to say about the great event at Bethlehem. Perhaps you are familiar with Jesse Tree symbols which represent Old Testament people, the forerunners of Christ. A tree so adorned becomes a family tree of the Lord. But the range and meaning of these figures may be a little beyond the younger children in a family—and so the symbols of *The Bethlehem Tree* are taken solely from the essential Christmas story. This is a beginning book of sign.

Each symbol is first presented for the parents' consideration; they can then tell their children why a particular ornament belongs on the tree, or provide in their own words a setting, a reason, for other suggested projects.

Not all ten decorations need be made for this Christmas! In fact, families might like to concentrate on one, making several of a kind for gifts. The home-made Christmas ornament is a satisfying present for a child to give: it is used and enjoyed by all, not put away in a drawer as a treasured keepsake. Everyone likes to see the work of his hands appreciated.

With the increasing secularization of "the holiday season," we can easily get lost on the way to Bethlehem. Let us not worry about a pressured world that begins a countdown of shopping time well before Thanksgiving. Instead, let us look for happy ways to illumine the birthday of the Lord so that our children will always know in their hearts the why of it.

WHY DO WE HAVE A CHRISTMAS TREE?

A tree is the oldest and most beloved of symbols. From ancient days, men have reverenced the tree for its tremendous vitality, its strength, its yearly renewal. It has come to be a sign of the holy, a Tree of Life.

Many cultures have chosen a particular Tree of Life. Many religions have worshiped beneath special trees and in sacred groves.

9

The banyan is holy to the Hindu;
the bo tree to the Buddhist;
the sycamore to the Egyptian;
the laurel, olive, and cypress to the Greek;
the peach tree to the Chinese;
the palm to the Phoenician;
the oak to the Druid;
the ash for the Teuton—
and there are many more.

In Israel's Golden Age, when Solomon built his magnificent temple, the huge beams to support the roof were cut from the famous cedars of Lebanon, standing (as they do today) one hundred feet tall. Within the holy place, a golden lampstand, patterned after a curving almond tree, lifted its arms like those of the people in prayer.

The Bible itself is called a Tree of Life. And the Bible begins with the story of a tree, a Paradise Tree that caused the close of Paradise—while the New Testament comes to a climax with the Tree of the Cross, a tree destined to reopen Paradise.

In medieval times, the Paradise Tree of the Book of Genesis was featured in a German mystery play that dramatized the fall of Adam and promised a Redeemer to come. This was a very popular pageant, part of an Advent cycle of plays leading up to the feast of Christmas; it was performed in church where often the only stage prop to indicate the Garden of Eden was a little tree, bright with red apples.

When the mystery plays were no longer presented, the little Paradise Tree was welcomed into the home—to honor Adam and Eve on December 24 (once kept as their feast day) and to hail the new Adam on December 25, the Promised Redeemer, Lord of all Creation. The tree retained its traditional fruit, and gradually cookies and cakes were added to delight the children, and candles were placed at the tip of every branch. Behold the Christmas Tree!

Such a tree is first recorded in 1605 in Strasbourg. England welcomed the Christmas tree when Prince Albert, the German-born consort of Queen Victoria, set one up for his children in Windsor Castle. With the first German immigrants, the tree crossed the ocean to America.

In many parts of the world, the coming of a child was once celebrated with the planting of a tree. A Palestinian family would set out a fragrant cypress for a new daughter, a strong cedar for a son. (Years later, the grown-up trees might be cut to form the standards for their wedding canopies.) The Swiss today plant a pear tree for a girl, an apple tree for a boy. There are Mexican families who name the birthday tree, giving it the same name as the child.

No wonder genealogy is diagrammed as a branching family tree. No wonder it is written: The just man shall flourish like a palm tree, like a cedar in Lebanon shall he grow.

Our Christmas tree then gathers together many traditions, unifies many themes, and sums up history from the beginning. It stands as a great sheltering Tree of Life over the Child in the crib. It is a Paradise Tree with shining fruit, a family tree extending its arms, a birthday tree glowing with birthday lights, an evergreen canopy celebrating the wedding of God and man.

> **Then shall all the trees of the forest
> exult before the Lord, for He comes,
> He comes to rule the earth.**
> **Psalm 96**

May your Christmas tree shout for joy at the coming of the Lord!

FOR YOUR OWN PARADISE TREE

The small colorful lady-apple, found in grocery stores at holiday time, is light enough to use as a tree decoration, an apt reminder of the early history of the Christmas Tree —which is still called a Paradise Tree in some corners of the world.

To suspend a lady-apple as a tree ornament, you will need a dressmaker pin (straight pin with round colored head— red or yellow will blend in well in this case) and a short length of either nylon filament or fine gold cord. Push the pin halfway into the top of the apple. Double the cord, knot the ends, loop-tie around the pin, then push the pin all the way down, leaving the rest of the loop for a hanger catch.

Something To Talk About

Which tree would you like for your birthday tree?

Trees are the oldest things alive. The giant redwoods are 3,000 years old; the bristle-cone pines are over 4,000. They were growing long before the first Christmas.

What do you suppose is pictured on the Lebanese flag?

Did you ever take part in a tree-planting or an Arbor Day celebration? In Israel, Arbor Day is known as the New Year of the Trees, and it is a special holiday. Nebraska is called the Tree-Planter State because on our first Arbor Day in 1872, Nebraskans planted one million little trees to shade their wide prairie.

Who was Johnny Appleseed? He was a very real person named John Chapman who wandered through the heart of our country, planting the seeds of future orchards.

> **"He has no statue,**
> **He has no tomb.**
> **He has his apple trees.**
> **Still in bloom."**

(*A Book of Americans* by Rosemary and Stephen Vincent Benét, New York: Holt, Rinehart and Winston, 1961)

Something To Read

A Tree Is Nice   by Janice May Udry (New York: Harper & Row, 1956); this received the annual Caldecott Medal for outstanding illustration.

A Tree for Me   by Norma Simon (Philadelphia: J. B. Lippincott, 1964); the story of a five-year-old who does indeed receive a birthday tree.

A Tree Is a Plant   by Clyde Robert Bulla (New York: Thomas Y. Crowell Crocodile paperback, 1973); one of the publisher's Let's-Read-and-Find-Out Science series.

A beginner's book of tree identification is a fine family Christmas gift.

Parents may wish to send for the government pamphlet, "How To Buy a Christmas Tree" (stock number 0100-

1518) available from the Superintendent of Documents, U.S. Government Printing Office, Washington, D.C., 20402, for fifteen cents. It describes kinds of Christmas trees and gives care and safety hints.

Something To Do

Search out special Christmas trees and Christmas cribs for the family to visit. Often a nearby town—or a neighbor—will have a memorable and unusual Christmas display.

New York's Metropolitan Museum of Art has a breathtaking tree. Its branches are brilliant with a host of 18th-century Neapolitan angels, in gold and velvet robes. Surrounding the tree are shepherds, townspeople, and kings, on their way to find the Madonna and her Child. The figures are from the collection of Loretta Hines Howard who each year directs the setting up of this Christmas gift to the city. The tree remains in place for some time after Christmas, hap-

pily for post-holiday visits.

The Franciscan Monastery in Washington, D.C. arranges an unforgettable life-size manger scene.

In Bethlehem, Pennsylvania, the Moravian Church has a Christmas crib that is nationally known. Visitors come a great distance to see the hand-carved mahogany figures in an elaborate landscape combining rural Pennsylvania and ancient Palestine.

We speak of a crib, a manger, a stable . . .
    but in France, it is the crèche;
    in Germany, it is the krippe;
    in Italy, it is the presepio;
    in Spain, it is the pesebre;
    south of the border, it is the nacimiento;
    and the Moravians say the putz.
What does your family say?

A TIME OF PEACE

In the forty-second year of the reign of Oc-
tavian Augustus, the whole world being at
peace, Jesus Christ, the eternal God and
the Son of the eternal Father . . . was born
in Bethlehem. (Liturgical Proclamation by
Dionysius, 6th century Divine Office for
Christmas Day).

For forty-five years, Octavius ruled the Roman Empire as great Caesar Augustus. This extremely long reign was a time of relative peace: fields were planted and reaped, towns and villages grew, trade flourished. Grain, olive oil, wool, leather, gold and silver, spices, amber, ivory, linen, cotton, and marble poured into the Empire on those long straight Roman roads—the same roads on which the Roman legions more frequently marched out to war.

In a time of absolute peace, it was customary to close the doors of the Temple of Janus, the god who has given his name to January. But this did not happen often. In fact, in the whole history of the Empire, the doors were closed only nine times. Three of these occurred in the reign of Augustus. And in one such period was born Jesus, the Prince of Peace.

Caesar's peace, however, was a Roman peace, one imposed on subordinates by a stern ruler, a peace laid on conquered people, a peace by law. This was the famous Pax Romana.

But Bethlehem's Child was to bring a different kind of peace, a peace from within, a peace of the heart—a peace that most of the world is still hoping for.

(Mothers and fathers know there are times, even in the Christian era, when they must continue to impose a Roman peace on a young household!)

Do we have any symbols to designate this longed-for age of peace? Artists have given us several interpretations of their vision of a peaceable kingdom when all creation will be in harmony and "the lion will lie down with the lamb" (Isaiah 11:6).

Perhaps our most familiar sign of peace is the dove, a symbol going all the way back to Noah and his great houseboat, the Ark. When Noah released the dove for a test-flight after the long voyage, it returned with a green olive branch. The chaos of the flood was over; the waters had receded; land and sea and sky were again reconciled. On the next time out, the dove did not return: it had found a new home on the dry land of new beginnings. Ever since, the dove has been a sign of peace to the world.

May the peace of the Lord be with you!

A DOVE FOR YOUR TREE

Materials: .

white card paper *or* any heavyweight draw-
    ing paper—8 ½ by 11 inches
tracing paper
gold paper of any kind (a very small
    amount)
scissors
paper punch
glue
medium gold cord for hanging—about 20
    inches

This is a cut-out-and-fold figure for older
children.

First make a pattern by tracing the dove in
this book, penciling lightly. Paper-clip the
tracing paper to the page. Note the two fold
lines. Cut out the pattern you have drawn.

Fold the white paper in half. Place the pattern on it; fold lines at the fold. Draw
around the pattern. Cut out the folded dove,

but do not cut the fold lines. (One is the top of the dove's head; the other will form the body.)

Make the indicated cut beside the dove's head. Bend the body section, with the second fold line, gently to each side, making a horizontal crease, a crease which begins at the bottom of the vertical cut.

Now open the folded dove to a single sheet. Reverse the body fold but *not* the head fold. Pull the body down inside the wings, against the horizontal creases. Bring the two sides of the dove together again.

Make gold circles for the dove's eyes with the paper punch and glue to each side of the head.

For a hanger catch, double the length of cord and knot ends. Loop over tail section, down under wings on each side, and up back of head. Draw the remaining doubled cord through the loop—(same principle as the pull on a window-shade.) Adjust the

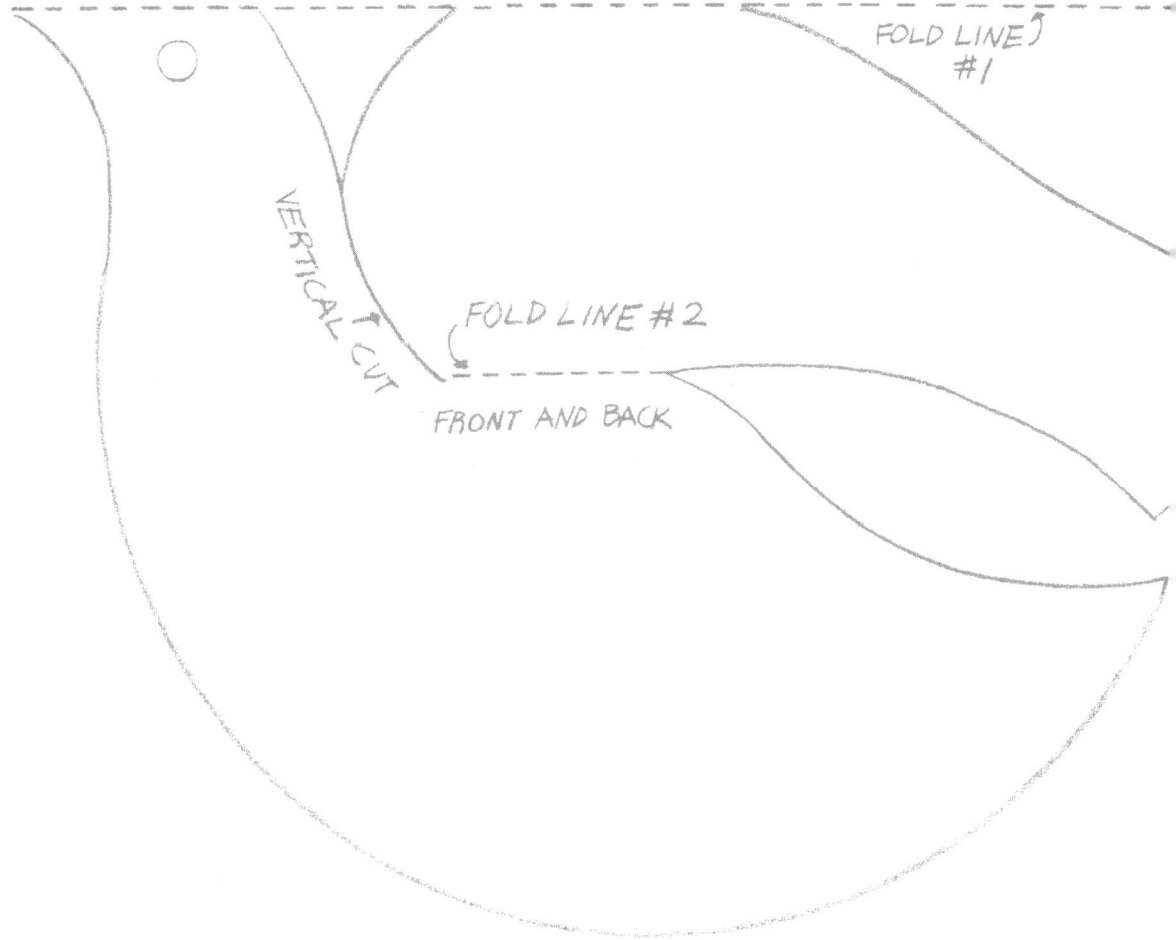

FOLD LINE
#1

VERTICAL CUT

FOLD LINE #2

FRONT AND BACK

24

cord so that the knotted ends are beneath the dove's body. The loop not only provides a hanger catch, but also keeps the body of the dove together while the wings flare out realistically.

WHERE TO FIND MATERIALS

Card paper is a very lightweight cardboard; it is the material used in most greeting cards. It is sold by the sheet in art stores, craft stores, and some stationers and printers. Ask for bristol board, 2 ply. Both the matt finish and the high gloss finish are attractive for this ornament.

Heavyweight drawing paper, heavier than the usual construction paper, can be found in dime stores in packs of many colors, including black and white. It has a smooth hard finish.

Lightweight typing paper or second sheets make good tracing paper.

So little of the gold paper is needed that it would be worthwhile to find an old sheet of used Christmas wrapping paper, or the back of a gold Christmas card. Save large metallic cards; they will often provide more than enough material for an ornament.

Medium gold cord will be found in gift-wrapping departments of dime stores, card shops, etc.

Something To Talk About

An ancient legend relates that for one hour on Christmas
Eve, all the animals can speak.

If the dove is a symbol of peace, are there other creatures
that are signs for us? Can you add to this list?

lion—kingly strength
bluebird—happiness
butterfly—transformation; new life
eagle—authority, power
mouse—timidity, "quiet as"
owl—wisdom
bee—"busy as"
lamb—gentle innocence
robin—spring is here
elephant—long memory, big!

Something To Read

There are many fine stories based on Noah and his Ark. A version that both parents and children will enjoy for its wit and verse structure is *Captain Noah and His Floating Zoo* by Michael Flanders (Indianapolis: Bobbs-Merrill, 1972).

See also *Noah and the Rainbow* retold by Max Bollinger, translated by Clyde Robert Bulla (New York: Thomas Y. Crowell, 1972).

And then there is *Why Noah Chose the Dove* by Isaac Bashevis Singer, with its brilliant pictures by Eric Carle (New York: Farrar, Straus & Giroux, 1973).

A dove brings peace, this time to the jungle, in *All the Animals Were Angry* by William Wondriska (New York: Holt, Rinehart and Winston, 1970).

The Box with Red Wheels by Maud and Miska Petersham (New York: Macmillan Collier Books, 1973—an old favorite reissued in paperback) is a gentle little story for small children about a baby's "peaceable kingdom."

Families who like poetry will want *Prayers from the Ark* by Carmen Bernos de Gasztold, translated by Rumer Godden (New York: The Viking Press, 1962.) Here Noah and his animals speak for themselves. A companion volume is *The Creatures' Choir*; both were issued as Viking Compass paperbacks in 1969.

Something To Do

Look through your Christmas cards for artistic doves; find also friendly lions and fearless lambs enjoying each other's company. Let the children mount these on construction paper for the family bulletin board.

"The Peaceable Kingdom," one of Edward Hicks' many interpretations of his favorite book theme, is available in poster size from the Book Shop of the Brooklyn Museum of

Art, Eastern Parkway and Washington Avenue, Brooklyn, New York. This might be an interesting Christmas gift for a child's room; be sure to place it low enough so that the animals can be named and enjoyed.

Every child should find a Noah's Ark under the Tree on at least one Christmas morning!

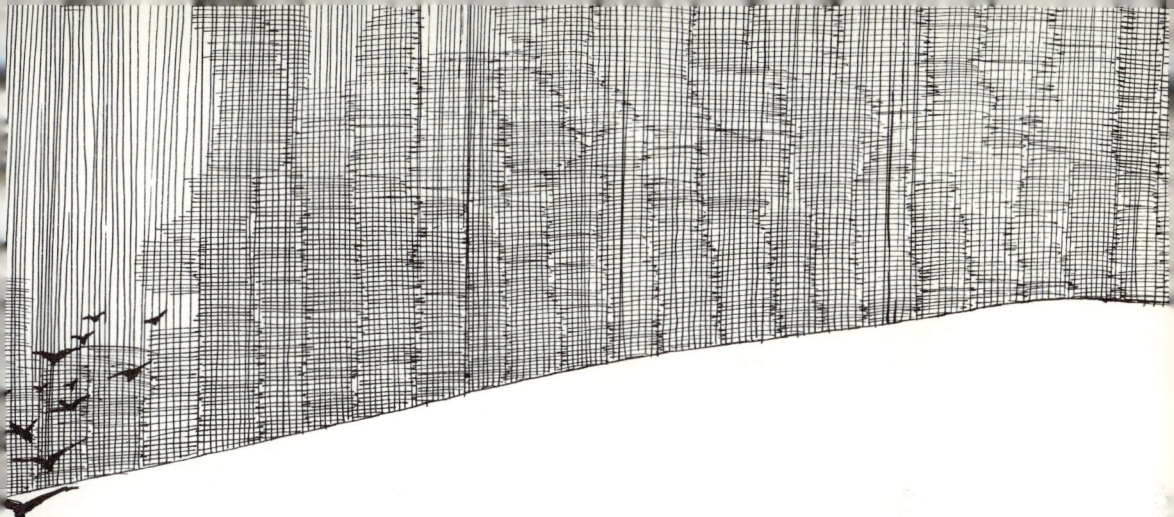

A FIELD OF WHEAT

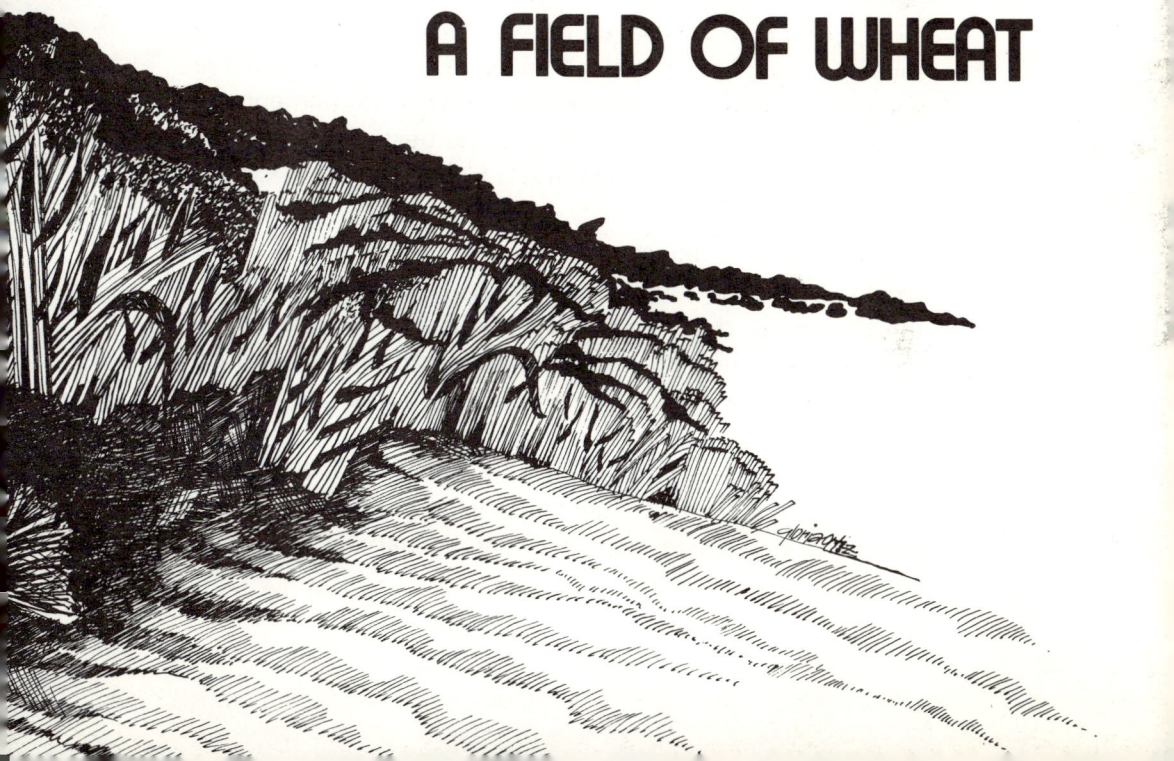

Below the carefully terraced hills of Bethlehem, where olives, grapes, and pomegranates grow, the valley stretches with fields of wheat and barley. Whether or not these gave the town its name, it is beautifully right that Bethlehem means House of Bread. (Beth . . . house; lehem . . . bread).

Fine wheat bread was a luxury in both Old and New Testament times; everyday bread was made from barley. The most fertile land was saved for wheat which was precisely sown in rows, after the fall rains, while barley and rye were sown broadcast, where the soil was not rich enough for wheat. "I would feed you with the best of wheat," the Lord says to his people (Psalm 81:17).

During the growing season, the farmer worried if there would be enough rain, if locusts would plague his crop, if the desert wind would swoop down to burn the young shoots. Harvesting in the spring was hard work: the grain was cut with a curved sickle and bound into sheaves for the threshing floor. Threshing was done on a high point of land to catch the wind; "the floor" was of rock or hard earth. Often several landowners held this area jointly, and owners and workers slept here during harvest to protect the grain.

To separate the kernels, the sheaves were beaten, or trampled under an ox-drawn sledge. Then the wheat was tossed into the air, into the wind ("winnowing"), to blow away the chaff and let the heavy grain fall down to be gathered.

Finally, to make the wheat into bread—but that is another story! No wonder that after all this, the end of harvest was a great festival time, with much feasting and celebration.

Long before the birth of Jesus, his ancestor, a young widow named Ruth, came to glean in the harvest fields of Bethlehem, that is, she was allowed by the landowner to pick up what was left after the reapers had gone through. This was the right of poor people, according to the Law. And after the poor, sheep were led in to find anything remaining. Nothing was wasted.

Ruth was the beautiful daughter-in-law of Naomi to whom she made her loving pledge of devotion: "Wherever you go, I will go. . . . Your people shall be my people, and your God my God." This young Gentile later became the wife of the kindly landowner, a true Cinderella story—and eventually she was the grandmother of Jesse (whence the Jesse Tree) and the great-grandmother of King David. David too was born in Bethlehem.

There are many levels of meaning in the small sheaf of wheat we will make for the Bethlehem Tree—a crescendo that builds to the Eucharist. The Child who was born in the House of Bread, who was laid in a manger of waiting grain, was to give himself as our food.

But for small children, perhaps it is enough to describe the little town on a hill with bright fields everywhere around it.

Blessed are you, Lord, God of all creation. Through your goodness, we have this bread to offer, which earth has given and human hands have made. It will become for us the bread of life.

Offering of the Bread

A SHEAF OF WHEAT FOR YOUR TREE

Materials:

6 wheat stalks
red, green, or gold yarn—approximately 18
    inches
gold or silver card paper, double-faced—3
    inches by 8 inches
scissors; ruler
paper punch
thin gold cord *or* nylon filament for hanging

The small sheaf will be mounted on a bright background to display it and facilitate hanging.

First trim the oblong of card paper to make a long oval. Make two holes in the center, side by side, with the paper punch.

Run the yarn through the holes, leaving the long ends in front.

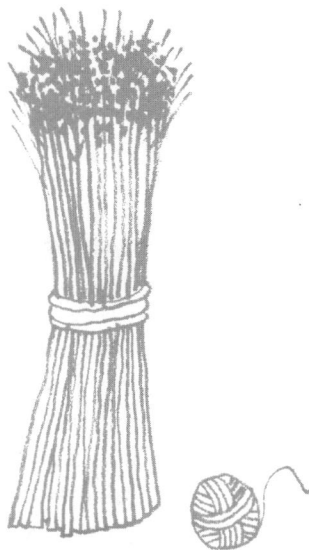

Place the wheat stalks on the card paper, and tie the yarn around them in a bow.

Trim the ends of the wheat evenly to measure, as a whole, 7-8 inches.

For hanging, double a length of gold cord or nylon filament, knot ends, loop through a small hole in the top of the card paper, drawing through as with a window-shade pull.

WHERE TO FIND MATERIALS

Where can you find real wheat? City folk can glean it at the florist's, and sometimes the dime store and supermarket. Large stores will carry it seasonally in the decorative flower department. Buy some for your Thanksgiving table and be ready for this Bethlehem symbol. It keeps for years (away from mice and birds).

Card paper is a very lightweight cardboard; it is the material used in greeting cards. You can buy sheets of it in craft stores, art supply stores, at some stationers and printers. The trade-name of one metallic card paper is Deco-Foil, supplied by Mangelsen's, Omaha, Nebraska, 68127. This comes in three double-faced sheets to a package.

The yarn should be of a good weight. It is often sold on cards in small quantities as a gift tie, in dime stores and gift-wrapping departments. Dime stores also carry short lengths of many-colored yarns for little girls' hair bows.

As for the hanging materials, thin gold cord is found in sewing shops and trimming departments, on spools or in packets, as 2-3 ply thread, as fine metallic cord, as metallic stretch cord, etc. It is often carried in craft shops.

Nylon filament, a single filament also called monofilament, is the almost invisible material used to hang most window decorations. It is sold in sporting goods stores as lightweight fishing line (leader material). You can, if you wish, buy it almost hair-fine. Although it is perfect for hanging ornaments, it is thin and slippery to handle. Younger children will need help in attaching their ornament loops.

Something To Talk About

Polish families begin their Christmas feast as soon as the first star appears on Christmas Eve. The dinner opens with the sharing of oplatek, an unleavened bread known as the bread of love. An extra chair awaits the unseen Lord—or any unexpected guest who may come to his place.

Eastern people sometimes lay straw beneath the Christmas table cloth as a reminder of the manger at Bethlehem.

In old Norway, it was the custom to spread fresh straw on the floor before any holiday. On Christmas Eve, the whole household slept together on the floor, in the new Christmas straw, to share the poverty and humility of the Christ Child.

Something To Read

For the youngest ones, a retelling of the story of the Little Red Hen will emphasize the long and wonderful process from seed-planting to bread-eating. See, for example, *The Little Red Hen and the Grain of Wheat* by Nova Nestrick (New York: Platt & Munk, 1961).

Another version is Paul Galdone's *The Little Red Hen* (New York: Seabury Press, 1973) although here unhappily the good bread has become cake.

Then there is Janina Domanska's *Little Red Hen*, dedicated "To all who will bake or eat bread" (New York: Macmillan, 1973). *The Tall Book of Nursery Tales* (New York: Harper & Row, 1944) also includes the story of this indomitable little barnyard mother.

Harold Berson's adaptation of an old tale, *The Boy, the Baker, the Miller, and More* (New York: Crown Publishers, 1974) introduces the many people behind one loaf of bread.

A perennial favorite for small children is Lois Lenski's *The Little Farm* (New York: Henry Z. Walck, Inc. 1970—a paperback).

For middle-grade children, the *Little House Series* by Laura Ingalls Wilder (New York: Harper & Row Trophy paperback, 1971) makes American farm life of the last century very real: the harvesting, threshing, and grasshopper plagues of almost biblical devastation. See especially *The Little House in the Big Woods, On the Banks of Plum Creek*, and *Farmer Boy.*

For older members of the family, there is a reference book with clear photographs and much information: *Wheat from Farm to Market* by Winifred Hammond (New York: Coward-McCann, 1970).

Something To Do

Shake out some of your wheat to find the chaff and the seed. Plant a few grains in a flower pot. Keep it moist. Store in a dark place for two or three days, then bring to the light and watch for the sprouts.

Pound a few of the grains to find the flour.

Try drinking through a section of the wheat stalk, the original straw. (Sometimes it works!)

Feel how rough and prickly are the "whiskers" of the wheat when you try to rub your fingers down them instead of up. They are like barbed arrows. Why do you suppose they are this way?

Read off the grains listed under ingredients on a rye or whole wheat bread wrapper.

If you have an old grist mill remaining in your area, pay it a visit.

Find Bethlehem, the House of Bread, on a map. How would you go there from Nazareth? How would you go there from Arabia? How would you go there from your town?

A man can live without spices, but not without bread.   The Talmud

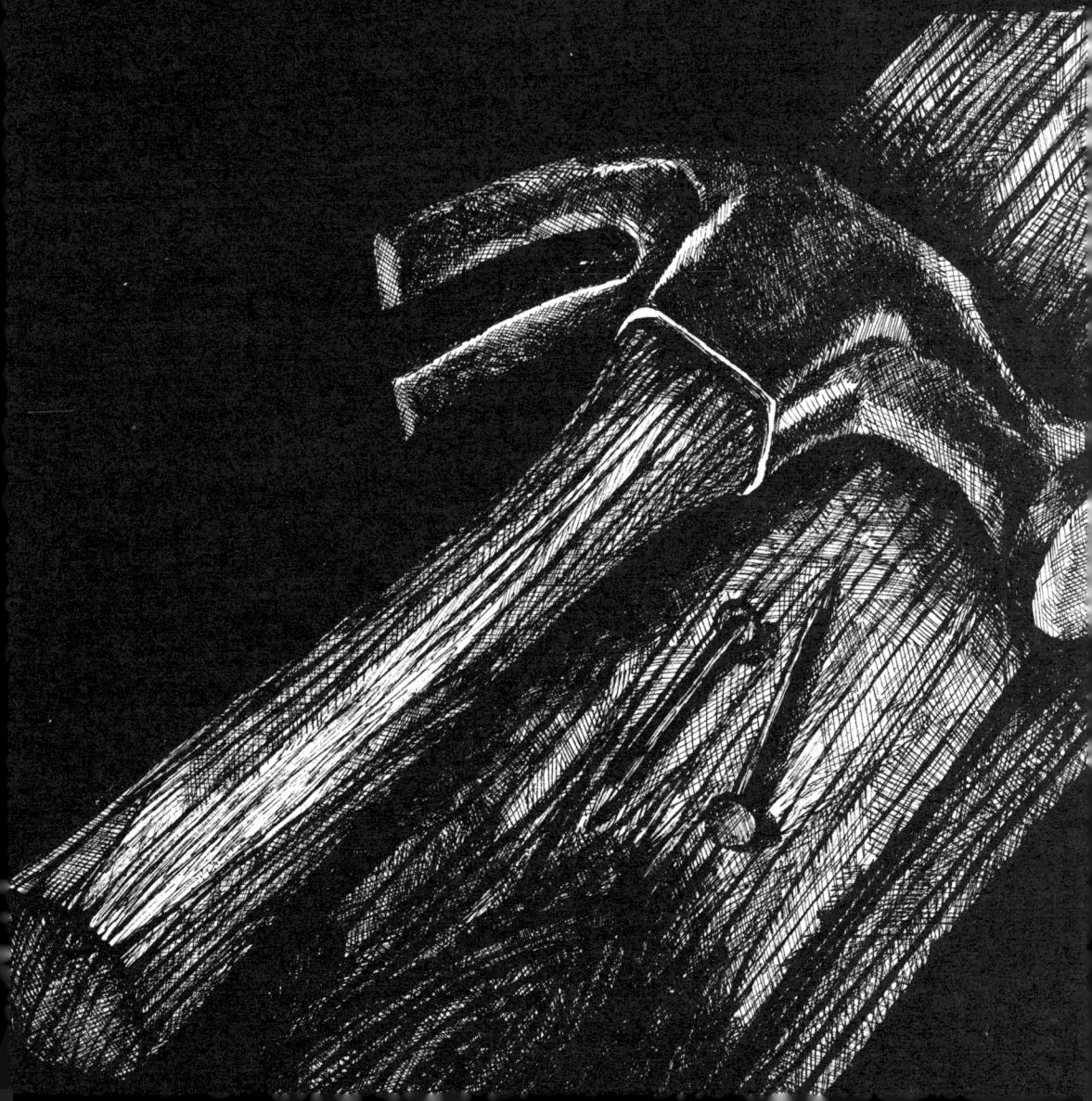

A TOOL
FOR A CARPENTER

The Christmas story begins when Joseph, the just man of Scripture, sets out with Mary, "his espoused wife who was with child," for Bethlehem, the city of their forebears, to be counted in a census. While today we expect a census-taker to come to us, in this instance the people went to the census-taker, going to their place of origin, their home town.

And on arrival in Bethlehem, there was no room for them in the inn.

(The inn was a caravansary of the type still existing in the East, a simple wall-enclosed space with one entrance and perhaps a few lean-to rooms along the wall for the well-to-do. The animals slept in the center, as did many of their owners with their cloaks about them. Naturally, it was a noisy, confused, and crowded place. Perhaps the quiet sheltered cave in the hill, with its waiting manger, was not such a poor second choice for this particular family.)

"And while they were there, the days for her to be delivered were fulfilled." So it was that Jesus was born in the home of his ancestors, in David's town, according to an ancient prophecy that Israel's new leader would come from Bethlehem.

Who was Joseph, the just man, to whom this long-awaited Child was entrusted? He was a young village carpenter, about the age of twenty.

What was his life in Nazareth like, as father and provider? His shop would have been part of his home, a one-room dwelling close to its neighbors. The floor would be of clay, and the roof would have strong wood rafters since the flat roof was also used as living space. A low wall, as the law decreed, ran around the roof, with a ladder or outside stair. Here the family often slept in summer.

Much of the work of the home could take place in the courtyard because of the mild climate. (Snow does sometimes fall in the Holy Land, so keep your white sheet beneath the Christmas crib!) This outdoor area served as kitchen—with oven for baking, and grinding stones for making flour. It provided a pleasant corner for meals, shaded by a grape arbor or fruit tree. And here was the carpenter's shop.

A village carpenter was kept busy with orders for doors, gates, rafters, stairs, and ladders; for ploughshares, bread troughs, storage chests; and, for those with homes large enough to hold them, such furniture as chairs, tables, stools, and benches. However, in most small houses, rush mats took the place of many furnishings.

Wood was not plentiful, especially construction wood. The carpenter probably had to find his own supply of wood and bring it home with the help of the family donkey. Sycamore was the usual building material, plus pine, cypress, and oak.

The tools in the shop at Nazareth would have included the ax, chisel, hammer, plane, drill, nails, and saw.

It must have been interesting for a small boy to grow up in

a home that was also a carpentry shop; there would be wood curls to play with, building blocks of all sizes, improvised boats and houses, perhaps whittled figures or whistles made in the carpenter's spare moments.

Joseph undoubtedly learned his trade from his father, Jacob, since crafts were hereditary. And carpentry was the trade he was to teach Jesus.

A carpenter who has no tools is not a carpenter.
The Talmud

Lord, give success to the work of our hands!
Psalm 90:17

A CARPENTER'S SAW FOR YOUR TREE

Materials:

gold or silver card paper, single or double-
    faced
tracing paper
glue
ruler
ball-point pen
pinking scissors
paper punch
nylon filament or thin gold cord for hanging

Transfer the saw pattern to tracing paper.
(Paper-clip paper to page.)

Place your drawing over an oblong of metallic paper, 3 inches by 6 inches. Go over
the lines lightly with a ball-point pen; the
metallic paper underneath will indent and
make it easy to cut out the saw.

(If the metallic paper is single-faced, with
white on the reverse, double the size of

OVERLAP HOLES

FOLD

"PINK" THIS EDGE

47

metallic paper and fold in half. Put the
dotted line of the pattern against the fold,
and draw as before. When you cut out, do
not cut the fold. Use a little glue to keep the
two sides of the saw together.)

Use pinking scissors to make a cutting edge
on the saw.

For a handle-grip, make three overlapping
holes with the paper punch.

To hang the ornament, loop-tie through the
handle with nylon filament or thin gold cord.

WHERE TO FIND MATERIALS

For metallic card paper and hanging materials, see notes
on the preceding ornament.

Light or medium-weight typing paper, and second sheets,
can be used for tracing paper.

Something To Talk About

Do you know someone whose shop is in his home, as Joseph's was?

Have you ever seen a wood curl made by a carpenter's plane? A long one might be an interesting ornament for the Christmas tree.

Long ago, a wood chip or wood curl was the sign of a carpenter's trade, and often he wore it behind his ear!

In India, a devout Hindu reverences the tools of his trade. He is taught to say a thankful prayer for pen or brush, hammer or hoe.

Something To Read

Preschoolers will like a picture book called *The Toolbox* by Anne and Harlow Rockwell (New York: Macmillan/Collier paperback, 1971).

But when it comes to using tools, a small child needs more than a book; he needs a teacher beside him. For parents and children, together, there are many good how-to books; one is Robert Lasson's *If I Had a Hammer* (New York: E. P. Dutton, 1974). It describes seven tools and details some simple projects for beginners (a bed for a pet, a hanger for potholders, etc.).

A House for Everyone by Betty Miles (New York: Alfred A. Knopf/Pantheon paperback, 1973) is a picture book, an excellent bedtime story, about the many varieties of home.

All About Houses by William Dugan (Racine, Wis.: Western Publishing Co., 1975, a Golden Book) has good pictures with much information and history.

Something To Do

Can you name the tools in the family tool-box?

Can you count the things in this room that were made by a carpenter?

Is there an image of St. Joseph in your church? Sometimes he holds a carpenter's square or saw to make sure you recognize him.

How many Josephs do you know, besides St. Joseph? Don't forget Giuseppe and José!

It is said that on the Sixth Day, God gave man tools—for his own creation.

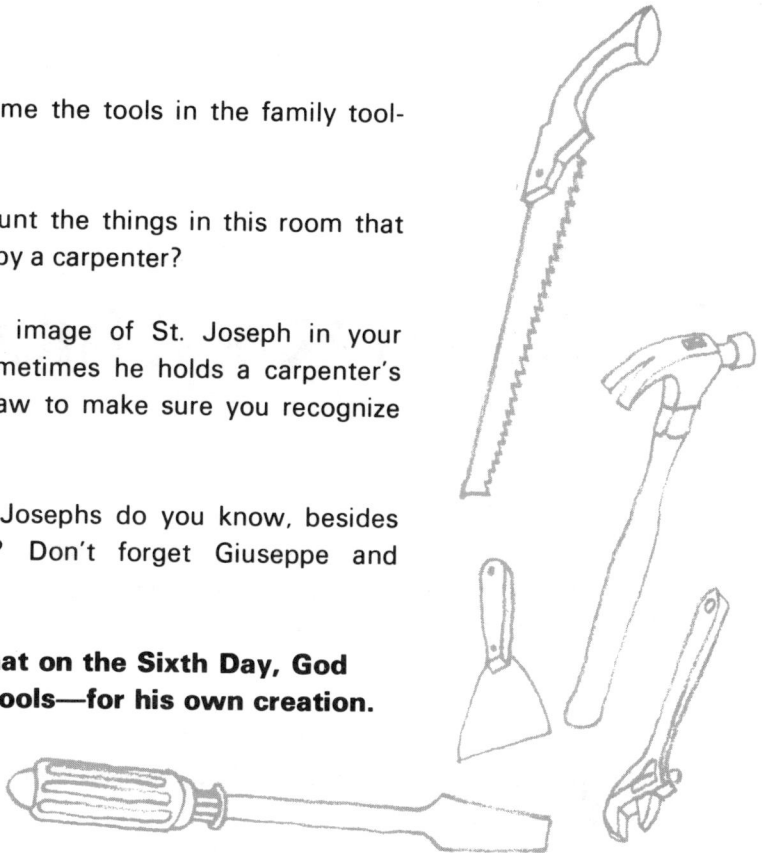

A SIGN FOR A MOTHER

What was it like to be a young mother in first-century Palestine? What was the daily life of a woman in Nazareth?

First and foremost, she was responsible for the food and drink of the household. Daily she carried water from the village well, balancing the container comfortably on a padded head-scarf. A Jewish home used a great deal of water for cooking and washing and also for purification.

Several times a week she would make flour, grinding grain in her own courtyard, using hand millstones. The sound of the grinding stones began the day in any village. She would make dough in her kneading trough and bake the bread outdoors in her cone-shaped oven.

She provided two meals a day, early and late, with perhaps a snack at noon. Meals were usually eaten outside. And they were good meals of fish and vegetables, of cheese and barley bread, of many fruits such as dates, berries, figs, grapes, melons, and apricots—and water, alone or mixed with red wine, stored in the coolest part of the house.

Every morning she would roll and store the bedding for the day. She would replenish the olive oil in the household lamp, a lamp that was never extinguished, but remained always lighted to insure a source of fire in the home.

She made her own cloth, spinning and weaving clothes and bedding. She washed clothes with her friends in the village stream.

The care of the children was hers. She taught them household ways. She taught them to pray; she taught them the meaning of the Sabbath and how to celebrate the festivals. Little boys would start school at the synagogue about the age of six. There under a teacher esteemed by the community, the children would begin their study of the Law by first learning the Hebrew alphabet.

In the evening, the mother enjoyed her flat open roof, talking with her family and neighbors and watching the children at twilight games.

What was she like, the young girl named Mary who was the Mother of the Lord?

We are fairly sure she was dark-eyed and dark-haired, and that she was indeed young: thirteen or fourteen was the usual age of marriage for a Jewish woman.

We know that in her presence one felt beauty, significance, sanctity, for an angel of the Lord exclaimed before her, "Hail, full of grace!"

We know she could be exuberant and joyful, running over the Judean hills to exult with Elizabeth in a God who kept his promises.

We know she was resolute, undertaking a difficult journey to bear her Child in the city of David, his ancestor. From Nazareth in the north to Bethlehem in the south is over ninety miles, a long rough way to travel.

We know she was thoughtful and reflective, keeping all things carefully in her heart.

The litany finds many poetic and symbolic titles for this mother: Lily of Israel, Cause of Our Joy, Mystical Rose, Tower of David, Tower of Ivory, House of Gold, Ark of the Covenant, Morning Star, Queen of Angels. . . .

But these lovely appellations demand some maturity of us, some background to appreciate them fully. Perhaps for a small child, the sign of this mother can well be a heart— for Mary is beloved of God, his valentine. Through her, God sent his Love to the world.

It is only with the heart that one can see rightly.
The Little Prince by Antoine de St. Exupery

A HEART FOR YOUR TREE

Materials:

red paper (card paper, metallic card paper,
    velour paper, heavyweight construction
    paper) *or* red felt
gold paper (card paper or foil wrapping
    paper)
scissors and ruler
glue
stapler (for variation only)
thin gold cord or nylon filament for hanging

A heart can be cut, freehand, from a folded
square. However, since this flat figure
should not have a fold in the center, first
make a heart pattern from any firm paper, 4
to 5 inches square. Trace around it and cut
out if using paper; pin and cut out if you are
using felt.

From gold paper, cut two wide curving letter
"M's". Glue to each side of the heart.

For a hanger, loop-tie with gold cord or filament through a small hole in the top of the heart.

A THREE-DIMENSIONAL VARIATION:

Cut four hearts the same size from red paper. These hearts *should* be folded in the center.

Staple the four together on the center crease, near the top. Loop-tie around the staple for a hanger.

When the hearts are opened up, the effect will be of a heart-apple. This, too, is a good symbol for Mary, the new Eve—and, like the lady-apple, reminds us of the original Paradise Tree.

WHERE TO FIND MATERIALS

For suggested papers and hanging material, see notes given with the first two ornaments. Velour paper will be found in craft shops.

Small oblongs of felt are sold in sewing shops, craft shops, fabric stores, and some dime stores.

Something To Talk About

Have you ever seen a well or tasted water from a well? To live near a well or a stream was once an absolute necessity: there were no underground pipes.

Have you ever slept in a sleeping bag? During the day, the "beds" of early homes were rolled up, just like sleeping bags.

Have you seen pictures of ancient lamps in school books or illustrated Bibles? A lamp was the warm, vital, ever-glowing center of the ancient home—its very heart, an inner sun. The poetic title given to King David and his descendants is filled with meaning: "Lamp of Israel." (And Jesus, Mary, and Joseph were of the House of David.)

Related to this was the belief of the medieval alchemists that the heart is the image of the sun within man—just as gold is the image of the sun within the earth. (Who were alchemists? They were long-ago scientists who attempted to turn ordinary metals into gold and who tried to find cures for all the ailments of humanity.)

And so we are discovering a new litany for Mary—as heart, as lamp, as image of the sun.

The name Mary comes from the Hebrew name of Miriam. (Remember Miriam, the sister who watched over little Moses in his reed basket?) Miriam is so ancient a name that we do not know its meaning. Some scholars think it comes from an even earlier Egyptian name that meant "beloved"—in which case our heart is a very good symbol.

Mary *is* beloved in every language: Moira, Marla, Maureen, Marya, Maria, and Marie. How many Marys do you know?

Something To Read

The Sky Was Blue by Charlotte Zolotow (New York: Harper & Row, 1963) is a book about mothers and the generations back of every child. In this, a little girl and her mother look at the family album together.

In My Mother's House by Ann Nolan Clark (New York: Viking Press Seafarer paperback, 1972) presents in poetic phrases the life of a Pueblo Indian child. Pictured here are flat-roofed homes, outdoor ovens, and grinding stones —as useful today as they were in Nazareth.

Something To Do

Find out where the water in your house comes from. If there is a nearby reservoir, take the family for a good look at it. And point out to the children where the water main enters your home.

You can make a little lamp with cooking oil and a floating taper to show the family how small a flame illumined early homes. To demonstrate, cut a thin circle from a cork, and cut out a similar round of aluminum foil to cover the top and keep the cork from scorching. Run an inch of candle wick through the center of both, letting the wick extend on each side. Place the assembled float in a small container of vegetable oil and light it—at night, in a dark room. For ages, a little dish lamp like this was the essential household fire. Even in our grandmother's day, such a vigil light was often used on home altars.

Scientists in the family may want to find out how long an ounce of oil will shine.

If Mary means "beloved," what does your name mean? Look in the dictionary. (Sometimes there is a *separate* section for proper names.)

TIDINGS OF GREAT JOY

An angel is a messenger of the Lord. That is the very meaning of the word; "angel" means messenger.

Traditions other than our own speak of angels. For the Arabian philosophers, angels were "intelligences." The Koran frequently mentions angels: they record man's deeds, accompany him in life, and transport his soul at death. The Greeks, however, thought of angels as distant "movers of heavenly spheres," far removed from everyday people and their small concerns.

In Scripture, it is an angel of the Lord who prevents Abraham from sacrificing his son. It is an angel of the Lord in a later age who leads the Hebrews to their Red Sea crossing and who protects them from the pursuing Egyptians.

The Archangel Raphael guards Tobias on his journey and enables him to heal his father's blindness. The Archangel Michael is the Lord's champion against evil and the special defender of the people of God. The Archangel Gabriel interprets the visions of Daniel and announces the coming of John the Baptist. And Gabriel is the angel of the Annunciation.

(Angelic names have meaning. Raphael signifies "The Lord heals." Michael means "Who is like the Lord?" And Gabriel means "God is my strength.")

Further, it is an angel of the Lord who reassures Joseph before he takes Mary as his wife, who later warns him to flee with his family to Egypt, and who eventually brings word that they may return in safety to Nazareth.

It is an angel of the Lord who ministers to Jesus in his desert temptation and who is with him in his great suffering the night before his death. And it is an angel of the Lord who announces to startled women that the Lord has risen.

These are the radiant and intuitive beings sent to us as guardians and heralds; they move with immediate power to make known the will of God. Full of authority, their presence is dazzling. Often they must reassure the awe-struck: Do not be afraid! Fear not!

Such an image is far removed from the charming cherubs of museum galleries or the "little angels" of children's stories.

On the first Christmas Eve, a majestic messenger of this shining company proclaimed to shepherds on their night-watch:

Do not be afraid, for behold, I bring you good news of great joy which shall be to all the people, for today in the town of David, a Savior has been born to you, who is Christ the Lord. And this shall be a sign to you: you shall find an infant wrapped in swaddling clothes and lying in a manger.
And suddenly there was with the angel a multitude . . . praising God and saying, Glory to God in the highest, and on earth peace among men of good will.

This is a message for all time.

A MESSAGE FOR YOUR TREE

Materials:

gold or silver card paper *or* foil paper
   (single-faced)
ruler
scissors
felt marking pen *or* a cut-out picture and
   glue
gold cord, 24 inches, medium weight

A shining scroll will represent the angel's message.

Cut a piece of metallic paper, 4 inches by 5 inches. The paper should be white on one side so the scroll can bear an actual message.

The message can be presented in several ways:

(a) a child can print with a felt marker: "The Lord has come!"
(b) a picture of the Christ Child, if possible

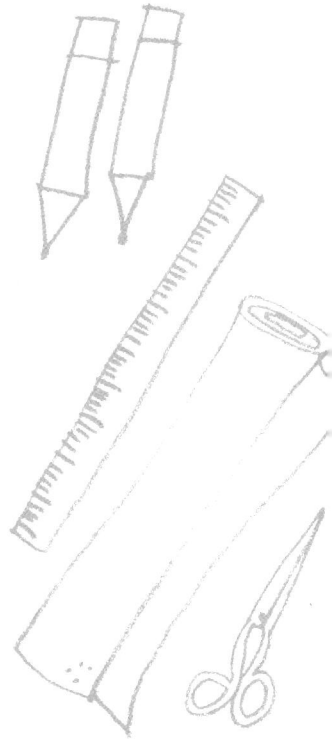

one in "swaddling clothes," can be cut out from a saved Christmas card and glued inside the scroll.

(c) simplest of all might be a child's drawing of the sun, the sign used in this book for the Lord, whose coming brought a new day to the world.

Roll up the scroll with its message inside. Now to tie it: Double the gold cord; tie around the scroll, crossing the cords once, not twice for a complete knot; make a bow of the loose ends, and use the looped end for a hanger catch.

WHERE TO FIND MATERIALS

For metallic card paper, see notes on the second ornament, in "A Field of Wheat."

Foil paper and medium gold cord are customary Christmas gift wrappings.

Something To Talk About

"You shall find an infant wrapped in swaddling clothes and lying in a manger." What are the swaddling clothes of the angel's message? They are the criss-cross wrappings of the newborn still used in many parts of the world. The terra-cotta baby in the familiar Della Robbia wreath wears these bands. Indian babies are laced to their cradle-boards with similar bands; propped against pueblo walls, they can safely and happily watch the family at work. (If you have a delicious German Christ-stollen at holiday time, notice how the dough has been criss-crossed— for a reason!)

Where did Los Angeles get its name? This town of the Angels, settled by the Spanish in 1780, was so-called for its bright skies and beautiful setting.

October 2 was designated the Feast of the Guardian Angels by Pope Paul V in 1680.

He will put you in his angels' charge
to guard you wherever you go.
Psalm 91:11

Something To Read (And Sing)

Messages can be given in many ways. All children will like *Talking Without Words* by Marie Hall Ets (New York: Viking Press, Seafarer paperback, 1968).

Tidings of great joy demand music. At the very beginning, the angel's message was told in song; it would be a strange Christmas without it. But don't take for granted that the children know all our lovely Christmas songs just because we do! An inexpensive and attractive booklet of eight carols, complete with music, is *And It Came To Pass*, Bible Verses and Carols selected by Jean Slaughter (New York: Macmillan Collier paperback, 1973.)

A much larger paperback is *A Treasury of Christmas Songs and Carols*, arranged for piano, voice, and guitar, edited by Henry W. Simon (Boston: Houghton Mifflin Co., 1973). It is nicely illustrated and has interesting notes about source, composer, etc.

Something To Do

Have you any family "swaddling clothes" put away: special baby clothes, baptismal garments! Children enjoy seeing your carefully kept reminders of their own long-ago.

What is a scroll? Diplomas were once presented as scrolls, tied with ribbon; now they come in flat cases. If you do have a rolled diploma or certificate (with its important message, its proclamation of good news), now is the time to show it and explain it.

The angel figure in a crib-set often bears a scroll. Does your Christmas angel tell the good news in this way? Can you read the words?

THE SHEPHERD'S CROOK

The shepherds who were keeping watch in the fields beyond Bethlehem were the first to come and find the Child. "They went with haste, and they found Mary and Joseph and the baby lying in the manger." Shepherds would have known every cave in their familiar hills; surely it was not hard for them to find the way.

Long before the first Christmas, David of Bethlehem looked after his father's sheep in these very fields. A shepherd was often the youngest working man in the family, as older brothers moved on to more demanding tasks. Large flocks, of course, required many experienced men (a flock of shepherds), but the few animals of a single family could be tended by one person, even a child.

The shepherd did not drive his sheep; he led them. He had to water them once a day. If the weather was bad, he gathered them in sheltering caves. If there was an injured lamb, he carried it. There were very real dangers: in desolate places, the flock had to be defended from jackals, foxes, bears, even lions in older times. A good shepherd might really be called to lay down his life for his sheep.

Sometimes a number of shepherds would meet in the evening, bringing their flocks together so they could take turns on the night watch and have companionship. And this is probably how it was on that first Christmas Eve.

Although different flocks might be quartered together at night, in the morning the sheep knew which shepherd to follow simply by his call.

He calls his own sheep by name and leads them out. . He goes before them and the sheep follow because they know his voice. . . . I am the good shepherd, and

I know mine and mine know me.

John 10:3-4, 14

In the fields, a shepherd would need a leather pouch and a gourd to carry food and water; perhaps a reed flute to pass the time; a warm cloak for cold nights; above all, a long curved staff, the age-old sign of the shepherd. This was indispensable for guiding strays back to the flock or bringing to safety a lamb caught on a ledge or in brambles.

The most familiar psalm in the Bible, traditionally composed by David, the shepherd-king, begins:

The Lord is my shepherd: I shall not want.
    In verdant pastures he gives me repose;
Beside restful waters he leads me;
    he refreshes my soul.
He guides me in right paths
    for his name's sake.
Even though I walk in the dark valley
    I fear no evil; for you are at my side
With your rod and your staff
    that give me courage.

When Micah, the Old Testament prophet, foretold that Israel's savior would come from Bethlehem, he phrased it

77

in this way: "Out of you will come a leader to *shepherd* my people Israel."

A SHEPHERD'S CROOK FOR YOUR TREE

Materials:

candy cane, medium size, 6-8 inches
gold self-stick decorator tape *or* mending
     tape (beige, light brown) *or* masking
     tape
scissors

Turn a candy cane into a shepherd's crook by wrapping it with tape. (Leave the cellophane wrapping on the candy cane, beneath the tape.)

Let smaller children use the candy cane for a pattern; they can trace and cut out a shepherd's crook from gold card paper or brown heavyweight paper.

Loop-tie with a thin hanging material, or let the crook loop itself over a tree branch.

WHERE TO FIND MATERIALS

Gold tape, including Scotch-brand Decorator Tape, will be found in dime stores, card shops, and gift-wrapping departments.

For gold card paper, heavyweight craft paper, and hanging material, see notes given with directions for the first two ornaments.

Mending tape and masking tape can be found in hardware stores and dime stores.

Something To Talk About

Even our nursery rhymes show that pasturing the flock was work usually left to the youngest in the family: besides Little Bo Peep who lost her sheep, there is Little Boy Blue who was caught napping when he should have been shepherding. Is there a particular chore for the youngest in your family?

Have you seen pictures of the golden image of King Tut, discovered some years ago in his Egyptian tomb? The boy pharaoh holds a blue and gold crook, a sign that he ruled a nation of shepherds.

Does a bishop's crozier have a familiar shape? It too is a shepherd's sign—for the shepherd of a diocese. Artists usually show the true St. Nicholas, the fourth-century Bishop of Myra, with his crozier, his shepherd's staff.

Although St. Joseph was a carpenter, he is sometimes represented with a staff because he is called the "Shepherd of the Church."

Christmas Midnight Mass is known as the Angels' Mass; the second at dawn is called the Shepherds' Mass.

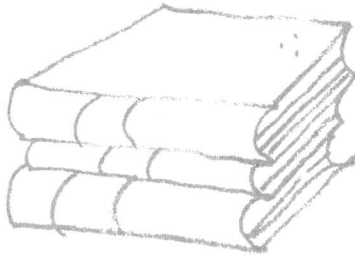

Something To Read

Parents who want to know something of the historical background and development of that famous fourth-century shepherd-bishop will find a complete account in *St. Nicholas, Life and Legend* by Martin Ebon (New York: Harper & Row, 1975). It is well researched and interestingly illustrated.

There are several fine editions for children of the Twenty-Third Psalm. One is Tony Palazzo's *The Lord Is My Shepherd* (New York: Henry Z. Walck, 1973, a paperback). Another is Marie Angel's *The Twenty-Third Psalm* (New York: Thomas Y. Crowell, 1970.) A third has Pennsylvania Dutch pictures: *The Lord Is My Shepherd*, illustrated by George Kraus (New York: E. P. Dutton Windmill Books, 1971).

A most appealing story about a real-life shepherdess is *Stephannie and the Coyote* by Jack Crowder (1970 paperback, Box 278, Bernalillo, N.M. 87004). Especially prepared for today's Navajo children, it is illustrated with excellent color photographs. ($1.50, postage included.)

Pelle's New Suit, a picture book by Elsa Beskow, translated by Marion Letcher Woodburn (New York: Scholastic Book Services, 1973, paperback) shows how the lamb gives his wool to become Pelle's suit—and it illustrates all the interesting steps in between: carding, spinning, dyeing, weaving, and sewing.

A book for older children about David, the shepherd boy of Israel, is *David and Goliath* by Beatrice Schenk de Regniers (New York: Viking Press, 1965).

Something To Do

Show the children some woolen mittens, sweaters, coats, caps, etc., so they can see how indebted we are to the sheep. People used to have a saying about someone or something very good: "All wool and a yard wide!" Have you noticed the symbol that manufacturers use on products that are 100% wool?

Our earliest portrayals of the Lord present him as a Good Shepherd with a lamb on his shoulders. St. Leo's League (Box 577, Newport, R.I. 02840) has a modern Good Shepherd in color by Ade Bethune, as well as a black and white Holy Family print, showing St. Joseph at work with his saw. These are a good size, suitable for framing. The League also offers small plaques of name saints and a stained glass dove for a peaceful window—all unusual and appropriate Christmas gifts. (St. Leo's League is a non-profit educational institution in Christian art and liturgy.)

THREE CROWNS

The Magi who traveled to Bethlehem were wise men of a priestly caste of scholars. Did they come from Persia, or Babylonia, or Arabia, the land that gave them their gifts? St. Matthew does not say; he only writes, "Behold, Magi came from the East."

Because of their great learning—in science, medicine, astrology—the Magi were regarded with awe as magic-men, in fact, magi-cians.

By the Middle Ages, the unnamed Wise Men of the Bible had become Gaspar, Melchior, and Balthasar, and they had been transformed into kings, three in number. (Other traditions give them other names, and there are twelve Wise Men in many Eastern countries.) Over the centuries, artists have continued to picture them as ermine-robed, golden-crowned, followed by a rich retinue.

If you visit the great Gothic cathedral of Cologne, where the Magi have always been venerated, you will see their glowing shrine on the high altar, and you can find Stephan Lochner's famous altarpiece, Adoration of the Magi, clear colors still shining, in the Lady Chapel.

The Gospels were written to proclaim the Lord as Savior and Messiah, to show that in him all the prophecies are fulfilled. In the story of the Magi, this purpose is especially evident: here faraway kings, wise men, the sages even of pagan lands, come before the Child to prostrate themselves, forehead to the floor, in Oriental homage. (Falling down, they worshiped him—Matthew 2:11.) For this is the Messiah-King, the Promised One of all time. He is the heart's desire of wise men everywhere.

The shepherds found the child in familiar hills. The shepherds were the Lord's own people, men of Bethlehem, men of King David's city. But the Magi represent the multitude who come from afar, across great stretches of time, to find him in unexpected places. In a way, they are there for all of us.

The kings of Tharsis and the Isles shall offer gifts; the kings of Arabia and Saba shall bring tribute. All kings shall pay him homage; all nations shall serve him.

Psalm 72:10-11

THREE CROWNS FOR YOUR TREE

Materials:

gold paper braid, 24 inches by
    approximately ½ to 1 inch width
gold card paper (small amount)
scissors and ruler
glue
nylon filament or thin gold cord for hanging

Make three of the following small crowns. Place them near each other on the tree.

Cut a 7-inch length of gold paper.
Glue ends together with a slight overlap.
This is the basic crown circle.

For a cap to the crown, cut two gold card-
paper strips, 1/3 by 4 inches. Attach these,
like basket handles, inside the crown circle,
at right angles to each other, crossing on
top. Glue the four ends of these strips to the
crown circle, overlapping well.

For a hanger catch, loop nylon filament or
thin gold cord under the crossed bands.

Crown variations can be made by using
different kinds of paper braid, by attaching a
narrow filigree band to a gold card-paper
circle (use transparent tape), or by jeweling
a card-paper crown with tiny beads,
sequins, etc., held with a touch of glue.

WHERE TO FIND MATERIALS

Several varieties of gold paper braid, used in decoupage,

will be found in craft and party shops.

For gold card paper and hanging materials, see notes given with the second ornament (A Field of Wheat). Double-faced gold card paper is better for this ornament than single-faced, but either will do. (Have you saved a metallic Christmas card you could use?)

Something To Talk About

What is the meaning of a crown? It has always been a sign of preeminence, nobility, sovereignty. But a crown is heavy. It also signifies the weight of responsibility. To wear a crown is to respond to trust.

Eastern rite families will be familiar with the symbol of the crown: their bishop wears a crown in the liturgy. So do their bride and groom in the wedding ceremony.

Many saints have also been rulers of their lands, wearing both crown and halo. Consider England's Edward the Confessor, Margaret of Scotland, Elizabeth of Hungary, Louis

IX of France (for whom the city of St. Louis is named) and King Stephen of Hungary, whose original crown is still the sign of sovereignty for Hungarians.

Is there a Stephen or Stephanie in your family? The name means "crown," from the Greek word "stephanos."

When was the last royal coronation? In 1969, Prince Charles of England received his coronet as Prince of Wales, from the hands of his mother, Queen Elizabeth. In 1971, the Shah of Iran (Iran is ancient Persia, considered by many the home of the Magi) at his coronation, crowned first himself and then his queen. On February 25, 1975, at precisely 8:37 a.m., Birendra was crowned king of Nepal —a time carefully ascertained by the court astrologers.

In many Spanish countries, it is appropriately the Wise Men who, on the Feast of Epiphany, leave presents for the children as they journey to find the Child. Latin people boast the longest of Christmas seasons!

Something To Read

The Wise Men from the East by Mies Bouhuya (St. Louis: Concordia and New York: Paulist/Newman Press, 1969, joint publication, a Bibletimes Book) sees the Bethlehem journey through the eyes of a young attendant in the Magi's caravan. There are excellent background notes, maps, and striking illustration, including a picture of an Eastern inn or caravansary. For school-age children and their parents.

A fact book for the scientific child is *Camels, Ships of the Desert* by John F. Waters (New York: Thomas Y. Crowell, 1974, from the Let's-Read-and-Find-Out Science series). It reveals the camel as a remarkable beast with long eyelashes to keep out the sand and nostrils he can close against the wind. And he can drink 100 quarts of water at a time.

Something To Do

A golden paper crown to wear on Epiphany can be a happy reminder of the Feast of Kings.

A specially decorated crown cake to celebrate Epiphany is described and illustrated in *My Nameday, Come for Dessert* by Helen McLoughlin (Collegeville, Minn.: The Liturgical Press, 1962).

Children may want to practice the way in which Oriental people venerated their ruler: down on both knees, forehead to the floor—an impressive language of the body.

THE STAR

The Magi followed their guiding star across the Arabian Desert, seeking a newborn king. The star brought them to Jerusalem—and to a king of sorts named Herod. The travelers had come a long way; when they reached this capital city, they must have looked for some excitement, some rejoicing at their news, some measure of the great expectation that had sustained them through strange lands, long nights, and the white heat of desert noons.

Herod—satellite king under the Romans; half Jewish, yet hated by the Jews as a Romanizer; a tyrant who suspected everyone of conspiring against him (and who therefore eventually executed his own brothers, sons, and wife)— this was the man the Wise Men approached for aid in finding a new king.

Could it be these strangers knew something he did not? Herod quickly called for his own wise men and put the question to them: Have we any clues as to the birthplace of an expected Messiah?

The priests and scribes of the Jewish people, familiar with the Law and the Prophets, could answer him: Yes, the Prophet Micah had indeed written, "You, Bethlehem, too small to be among the clans of Judah, from you shall come forth . . . one who is to be ruler in Israel, whose origin is from of old, from ancient times" (Micah 5:1-3).

Making his own plans, Herod therefore directed the pilgrims south to the village of Bethlehem. He would come to pay homage once they had found this new ruler of Israel!

And again the star went before them and brought them to the Child, and there was an end to their long search.

Why did the star, symbol of divine guidance, direct the travelers to Herod, of all men? What is the meaning here? Perhaps it is that no one must be omitted, no one forgotten. Even an arch-enemy of the Child must be told, "He has come!" The invitation to welcome this king is extended to absolutely everyone.

If you were to follow the Wise Men and come to Bethlehem today, you would find not a little cave in the hillside, but the ancient Church of the Nativity, dating from the Crusades, erected on the site of St. Helena's original shrine and Justinian's later chapel. It has one small door, and all must enter it in single file, bending a little. You will learn that long ago an imposing entrance was walled up to prevent infidels from riding in on horseback to desecrate the holy place. But there are many meanings to the little doorway of Christ's Nativity.

Inside, you will descend stone steps to an underground grotto, its air heavy with incense, its smoke-blackened walls illuminated by a multitude of filigree lamps. Set in the floor is a great fourteen-pointed silver star; engraved in Latin, it reads: Here Jesus Christ was born of the Virgin Mary. At midnight on Christmas Eve, a figure of the Child is placed in the center of the star, and many symbols come together.

At thy birth
They who worshiped the stars
By a star were taught to worship thee,
The Sun of Righteousness . . .
                              Syrian Christmas Hymn

A STAR FOR YOUR TREE

Materials:

card paper in gold or silver, preferably double-faced *or* a
    good weight of foil paper
paper fastener
scissors and ruler
nylon filament or thin gold cord for hanging

Cut two 5-inch squares from metallic paper.

With each:
(a) fold through the center to make right-angle cross lines.
(b) fold from corner to opposite corner to make diagonal
     lines (the purpose here is to give a three-dimensional
     look to the star).
(c) crease firmly, then open.

(d) on each cross-fold, mark one inch from the center.
(e) cut down from corners of the square to the 1-inch
      marks; cut away the triangles formed; this will leave
      a four-pointed star.

Join the two stars in the center with a paper fastener, thus
making an eight-pointed star.

For a hanging loop, double a length of filament or gold
cord and knot the ends. Loop-tie around the opened
prongs of the paper fastener, drawing through as with a
window-shade pull.

A variety of beautiful stars can be made by combining
gold, silver, and other metallic papers in various sizes;
stars with more "point" can be made by cutting closer to
the center. One fastener will join as many as four stars.

WHERE TO FIND MATERIALS

For metallic paper, and hanging materials, see the notes
given with the second ornament, "A Field of Wheat."

Something To Talk About

Are there other Bethlehem towns? There are at least three
others: one in Pennsylvania, one in West Virginia, one in
Africa. Pennsylvania's Bethlehem (often called the Christmas City) lights a great star on a high mountain tower, vis-
ible for miles, during the Christmas season.

Stars represent the states in our flag. In Israel's flag, there
is a six-pointed Star of David.

Estelle and Stella are "star" names. And Lucy, Lucia,
Clare, Eleanor, Eileen, and Helen mean "light."

Something To Read

Stars by Melvin Berger (New York: Coward, McCann & Geoghegan, 1971) is one of many good beginning books for small star-gazers.

Oasis of the Stars by Olga Economakis (New York: Coward-McCann, 1965) tells how a young boy finds water for his desert tribe. Readers will learn a great deal about nomadic people who can travel by the stars.

Something To Do (And One More Book)

In many parts of the world, Christmas carols are sung by children dressed as Wise Men who go from house to house, singing and re-enacting the journey to Bethlehem.

These "Star Boys" traditionally carry star lanterns. In Scandinavia, Star Boys first appear on St. Lucia's Day, December 13. In Alaska, "going around with the star" continues all Christmas week, and the carollers are often invited in for refreshments. Sometimes the Star-Boy Kings are closely pursued by Herod's men—which adds considerable excitement!

Your own home carollers might enjoy robing like the Magi and following a star on their rounds. A star wand is not hard to make—with a stick and one of our paper stars. And let the youngest carry a star as you bring the figures of the Wise Men— with some ceremony—to the crib on their feast of Epiphany.

Take the family outside to see the winter stars some December night. Think of the long ages during which men were able to travel safely and surely only because they knew the star patterns. Find Polaris, the constant North Star, an unchanging sign in the glittering skies.

Going out in the cold night to see the stars is an unforgettable experience for small children. A book that catches the mood (if not the season) is Charlotte Zolotow's *The Summer Night* (New York: Harper & Row, 1974). A good bedtime story for any time of year.

Star light, star bright,
First star I see tonight,
I wish I may, I wish I might
Have the wish I wish tonight!

I wonder if the Wise Men wished on their star. What is your star-wish this Christmas?

THE GIFTS

The very first Christmas gifts were gold, frankincense, and myrrh, carried across the desert in camel caravan, and presented by Wise Men to an infant in his mother's arms. Our children may think them strange gifts to give a baby! But wise men of other ages, poets and saints, have always found great meaning in these first Christmas gifts—the first birthday presents, too, for Bethlehem's Child.

GOLD FOR A KING

Our legends and fairy tales are aglow with golden apples and golden eggs, emperors and their golden birds, giants counting their yellow coins, galleons heavy with pirate treasure. Gold is the symbol for fabulous wealth and power. Every child knows this, even if he has not set eyes on one piece of it.

In the ancient world, this royal metal was used lavishly. Kings and courtiers wore massive bracelets, rings, brooches, earrings, and necklaces. The homes of the wealthy were adorned with vessels and figurines of solid gold. Gold deposits were, in fact, once so plentiful, especially in Egypt, that there was a time when silver was considered more precious.

In Israel's great Temple at Jerusalem, the lampstand was pure gold. The Ark, the Altar of Incense, the temple gates were all overlaid with imported gold—as was the throne of Solomon.

Fine linen was often interwoven with spun gold to make gleaming robes and vestments. In those days, a goldsmith may well have been busier than a blacksmith.

And Arabia's gold was considered the most desirable—a present fit for a king. In fact, all three of the Magi's gifts were from Arabia, regal and of great significance.

INCENSE TO GOD

Incense has always been beloved throughout the East. Centuries before Christ, a relief sculptured on an Egyptian wall shows royal gardeners carefully transplanting a little incense tree.

Rising and enveloping in its sweetness, the smoke of incense speaks of the transcendent, the holy. Its light fragrant cloud signified to Israel the presence of the Lord; it accompanied all Temple offerings. The Book of Exodus prescribes the exact ingredients for the special incense of the sanctuary: "Take sweet spices: storax, onycha, galbanum . . . and pure frankincense in equal parts. . . ."

Frankincense means the best of its kind—a genuine, fine, free-burning Arabian resin.

MYRRH FOR MAN

Myrrh is also a resin, from the bark of a thorny little Arabian tree. Although it has a heavy sweet aroma, myrrh has a bitter taste; its very name means "bitter." It was costly and precious up into the Middle Ages.

Myrrh was a valued ingredient in rare perfumes; it was blended in the anointing oil which consecrated priest and king—and which prepared the body for burial.

Myrrh is one of the oldest of medicines, and is still in use as an antiseptic and astringent. Often too it was mixed with wine to ease pain.

Myrrh therefore stands for the life and death of man, the sweetness and the anguish of man's existence. It dedicates his calling, his commitment.

And myrrh signifies healing for a people in need of it, in need of salvation, in need of a savior.

Caravans of camels shall fill you . . . all from Saba shall come bearing gold and frankincense, and proclaiming the praises of the Lord.

Isaiah 60:6

What they believe in their hearts, they proclaim by their gifts: they offer incense to God, myrrh to man, and gold to a king.

St. Leo's Epiphany sermon

KINGLY GIFTS FOR YOUR TREE

Materials:

gold netting—three 9-inch squares
gold-foil-wrapped chocolate coins
frankincense
myrrh
thin gold cord

This ornament consists of three small gift bags containing (almost) the original gifts of the Magi. Gold is represented by the foil-wrapped coins; actual "tears" of myrrh and grains of frankincense fill the other bags.

To make the bags, run a draw-string of gold cord around the netting square, in a circle

close to the edges. Leave long ends so that you can knot them for a hanging loop. Fill and close with draw-string. Place the gifts together on the tree.

WHERE TO FIND MATERIALS

The coins are chocolate novelties found in Christmas candy stores and often in the dime store. They are usually sold in gold mesh bags.

Gold netting, a fine metallic mesh, is stocked by large fabric stores and sometimes by trimming and craft shops. If it is difficult to find, buy extra "coins" to supply bags for all three gifts. Tulle in various colors can be substituted; it is an inexpensive fine-mesh nylon material sold in fabric shops. But it is second choice.

For thin gold cord, see notes on the second Christmas ornament: "A Field of Wheat."

Frankincense and myrrh can be obtained from
(a) Gift shops and herb shops. One supplier is Rocky Hollow Herb Farm, Sussex, New Jersey 07461. Available in plastic bags.

(b) Church supply stores.

(c) The Metropolitan Museum of Art, Fifth Avenue at 82nd St., New York, N.Y. 10028. Contact the Junior Museum Sales Department (the Folk-Art Shop.) Available in inexpensive small quantities.

(d) The Christian Family Catalog, Abbey Press, St. Meinrad, Indiana 47577, catalogue number 06258. Available for gift-giving in redwood canisters.

(e) The David C. Cook Catalog, 850 North Grove Avenue, Elgin, Illinois 60120, catalogue number 12401. Available in a small divided plastic box, packaging the two gifts together.

Something To Talk About

On Twelfth Night, it was once the custom in the English royal chapel to offer gold, frankincense, and myrrh, in the name of the Crown.

Medieval children received their Christmas gifts three at a time, to remind them of the three gifts of the Magi.

To be custodian of the incense is a very special assignment for an altar boy. Officially the censer is called a thurible; and so an altar boy is a thurifer!

A name that means "gift of God" is Matthew. So does John. So does Dorothy.

For Christmas of 1636, the great Black Robe missionary, Jean de Brebeuf, taught his small Hurons a carol in their own language. The kings have become Indian chiefs, and the gifts are their own.

Within a lodge of broken bark
the tender babe was found,
a ragged robe of rabbit skin
enwrapped his beauty round.
  And as the hunter braves drew nigh
  the angel song rang loud and high:
  Jesus, our king, is born!

The earliest moon of winter time
is not so round and fair
as was the ring of glory on
the helpless infant there.

**While chiefs from far before Him knelt,
with gifts of fox and beaver pelt,
Jesus, our king, is born!**

Translated by J.R. Middleton
(from *St. Isaac and the Indians*
by Milton Lomask
New York: Farrar, Straus
and Cudahy Vision Books, 1956)

Something To Read

What is a just-right gift? A book that wonders about this is Charlotte Zolotow's *Mr. Rabbit and the Lovely Present* (New York: Harper & Row, 1962). With help, a little girl finally decides on a gift for her mother. See, too, *The Happy Birthday Present* by Joan Heilbroner (New York: Harper & Row, 1962).

A collection of fairy tales, beautifully illustrated, is always a just-right gift for Christmas. In these door-openers to mystery and symbolism, every gift is endowed, with meaning, whether golden apple or handful of colored beans.

Lorenz Graham's *Every Man Heart Lay Down* (New York: Thomas Y. Crowell, 1946, 1970) tells the Christmas story in fresh poetic African phrases:

"And the king bring gold for gift,
and the wise man bring fine oil,
and the country people bring new rice. . . ."

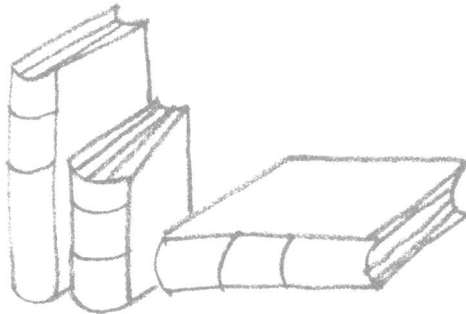

Something To Do

If you live near a city museum with exhibits of ancient jewelry, ornaments, etc., take the family (in some less pressured season!) to admire gold—in warm glowing quantity. You will begin to understand those fairy-tale misers and kings, those legendary heroes and their golden guests.

You don't need burning charcoal to smell frankincense. Simply place two or three grains in a metal spoon and heat slowly over a candle flame. Soon the resin will melt and begin to smoke, releasing its ancient aroma. Myrrh can be heated in the same way.

Remember on Christmas Eve that the Wise Men should be placed some distance from the crib. Let the children move the figures nearer each day, arriving on Epiphany, January 6, Twelfth Night, the Feast of the

Three Kings, the completion of the great Birthday Celebration.

Christmas, so long awaited, should have a happy and definitive close. Epiphany can be the day the Wise Men arrive and their story retold, the day on which all then help to dismantle the tree and put the ornaments carefully away. A simple festivity for children is a spice tea-party, with cloves in the lemon and cinnamon-stick stirrers—those spices of the Orient that used to come by camel caravan. Save the last of the Christmas cookies for this.

(Or perhaps aunts, uncles, or grandparents would like to become the traditional hosts for this final celebration of Christmas so that parents, like the Eastern kings, may rest after their long Advent journey.)

THE SUN

What shall be the sign of the Child, the one who was born at night, in the darkness of a hillside cave, in a forgotten, out-of-the-way corner of the Roman Empire? Let it be the sun in its brilliance, the day-star, the light of the world!

It was a fearsome thing for early earth-dwellers to see the days grow short and the dark shadow of winter lengthen. Would night descend completely and forever? Through ritual and sacrifice could this terror be averted?

And so the Persians kindled fires to Mithra, their god of light; the Egyptians worshiped their sun god, Ra, who was reborn each morning in the form of a child; and Teutonic people set enormous bonfires to stave off the darkness and herald the sun's return. (Their word, yule, means wheel, the great wheel of the sun.)

It was also at the time of the winter solstice that the Romans held their Saturnalia, a festival period in honor of an earlier Golden Age: schools were closed, people gave gifts to one another, and even the slaves feasted. On December 25, the close of these holidays, as the Emperor Aurelian decreed, all the citizens assembled to worship the "Unconquered Sun."

You will learn that it was not until the fourth century, in Constantine's time, that the feast of Christmas was celebrated throughout Christendom. You will read that the date was chosen to offset these many pagan festivals.

And Christmas did prevail. But this should not be seen as a replacement, a supplanting. More truly, Christmas is the culmination, the fulfillment, of all those ancient yearnings and solemnities. All previous celebration now shines with new meaning. The Birthday of the Sun becomes the Birthday of the Son—the radiant Dawn Child who illumines all people, even those before his coming.

Long before the time of Christ, an Egyptian pharaoh sang this hymn:

Beautiful is your rising in the horizon of heaven, Living Sun, you who were first at the beginning of things. . . . You fill every land with your beauty. Your rays embrace the lands to the limit of all you have made. . . . Only God, there is no one like you.

from Akhenaten's Hymn to Aten, the Sun (c. 1370 B.C.)

Long before the time of Christ, the Prophet Isaiah sang this hymn, to a Child who would be called Son of God and Son of Man:

The people who walk in darkness have seen a great light; upon those who dwelt in the land of gloom, a light has shown. You have brought them abundant joy and rejoicing. . . . For a child is born to us, a son is given to us; upon his shoulder dominion rests. And his name shall be called Wonderful, Counselor, God the Almighty, Father of the World to come, the Prince of Peace.

Isaiah 9: 1-2, 5(c. 735 B.C.)

A SUN FOR YOUR TREE

Materials:

gold card paper, single or double-faced
gold foil paper
ball-point pen
scissors
glue and Scotch tape
2 different-size glasses or jars for circle guides
nylon filament or thin gold cord for hanging

This sun is a golden disk with golden rays.

Cut two identical card-paper circles, 3-4 inches in diameter. To make the circle, draw around a small drinking glass, using a ball-point pen to indent slightly. It may be sufficient simply to press the rim of the glass on the paper. In the same way, make two larger circles of foil, 5-6 inches in diameter.

Join the circles with small drops of glue, the larger foil circles, back to back, between the smaller card-paper circles. The knotted end

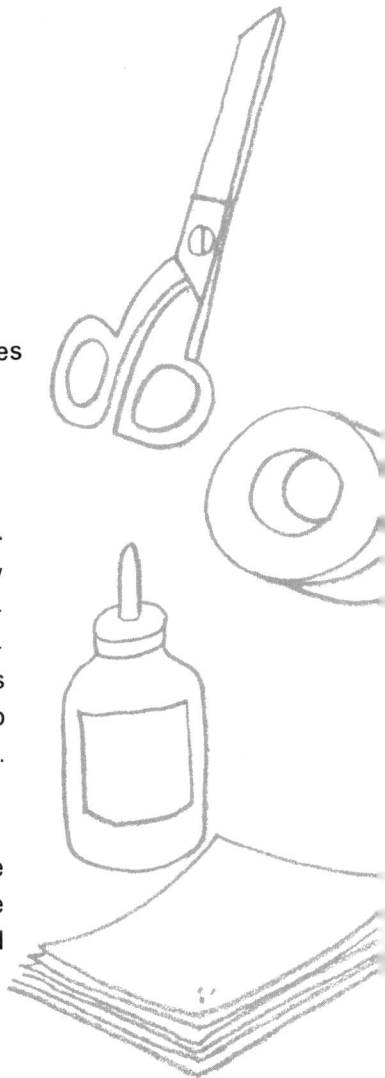

of the hanging loop should be taped in the center of one of the foil circles before assembling.

With scissors, fringe the foil circles in toward the gold disk center to make sun rays.

Older children can design a Chi-Rho, the ancient monogram for Christ, to emboss the sun disk. Use gold foil and cut out the letters (X and P) separately; it is easier to superimpose them than to cut the complete figure.

This symbol consists of the first two letters of the Greek word for Christ. It is an abbreviation, a short way to write a most special name.

The Chi-Rho is found on the walls, altars, and tabernacles of churches; it is embroidered on vestments and altar linens. Its Christian use dates from the time of Constantine.

But long before, it was a symbol of good

fortune for the Romans, a prophetic sign of
an unknown coming Good.

WHERE TO FIND MATERIALS

For metallic card paper and hanging materials, see the
notes given with the second ornament in "A Field of
Wheat."

Foil paper is readily available as a gift wrapping.

Something To Talk About

Helios was the name of the Greek sun-god, and Rhodes
was his special island. A colossal bronze statue of Helios
stood astride in the harbor, so large that ships in full sail
could pass between his legs. Naturally, he was counted
among the Seven Wonders of the World. (An earthquake
brought him down!)

The rising sun is the emblem on the Japanese flag. In old
Japan, sunrise was welcomed by handclapping.

Do you live in New Mexico? The Indian sign of the sun, the Zia, is on your state flag. The capitol at Santa Fe is also shaped like the Zia, with its four entrances signifying the four winds, the four seasons, the four directions, and the four stages of life, as do the rays in the sun-sign.

The Cheyenne people have always called themselves the People of the Morning Star, for to them and all Plains Indians, the sun is a sacred symbol for God. They wish to be known as God's own people.

The first day of the week is Sun-day.

Do you remember the rhyme about the child born on the Sabbath Day who was always "bonny and blithe and good and gay"?

Children love to hear the details of their own beginning— where they were born, on what day, at what time, who welcomed them, who named them, and why. Advent, the season of beginnings, when we make new the Lord's coming, is a good time to tell children again about their own Advent.

Something To Read

Among the great themes of Advent are anticipation— and waiting. For ancient people, waiting meant enduring the long winter until the sun's return. For Israel, waiting means an age-old longing for the Messiah. For Christians, waiting means living in hope of the Lord's return, a continuing Advent. For children, waiting means counting off the interminable days till Christmas. *I'm Waiting* by Myra Cohn Livingston (New York: Harcourt Brace and World, 1966) emphasizes the many things that must be awaited every day.

And then after Christmas, we must wait a whole year till it comes again! *The Day after Christmas* by Alice Bach (New York: Harper & Row, 1975) is about a girl who finds this very hard.

Dawn by Uri Shulevitz (New York: Farrar, Straus & Giroux, 1974) is a picture book about an old man and a boy waiting for the sun in the very early morning. It was inspired by a long-ago Chinese poem.

Arrow to the Sun, adapted and illustrated by Gerald Mc-

Dermott (New York: Viking Press, 1974, a Caldecott winner) is a Pueblo tale in which a boy seeks his unknown father, the Sun, source of all life. An allegory for all people.

Two informative little books by Franklyn M. Branley are *What Makes Day and Night* (New York: Thomas Y. Crowell, in Crocodile paperback edition, 1972) and *Sunshine Makes the Seasons* (New York: Thomas Y. Crowell, 1974). The author is chairman and astronomer at the Hayden Planetarium. Both books are from the publisher's Let's-Read-and-Find-Out Science series.

Signs and Symbols of the Sun by Elizabeth F. Helfman (New York: Seabury Press, 1974) gives some indication of what the sun has meant to the many people it shines upon.

Song of the Sun, St. Francis of Assisi's Canticle of the Sun, has been charmingly illustrated by Elizabeth Orton Jones (New York: Macmillan, 1952).

St. Francis is a special Christmas saint because he gave us the first Christmas crib. After a pilgrimage to Bethlehem in 1223, Francis arranged a life-size manger for the townspeople of Greccio. On Christmas Eve, they came through the woods by torchlight to see the new Bethlehem Francis had made for them.

St. Francis is the saint who counseled farmers to give extra rations to their animals at Christmas and to spread new hay in the stalls. He asked everyone to throw seeds where the birds could find them for their Christmas dinner. He wished all creation to celebrate the birthday of the Lord.

Two books about this saint who loved Christmas are: *St. Francis and the Animals* by Leo Politi (New York: Charles Scribner's, 1959) and *The Song of Francis* by Fray Angelico Chavez (Flagstaff, Ariz.: Northland Press, 1973) —for teens and adults.

Something To Do

Find a sun-dial (in a garden, in a park, in a museum, or in a landscape supply store). See if you can tell time by it.

Are there any plants in your windows? Which way do the leaves turn?

Plant a few sunflower seeds next spring. In the summer, watch how the sunflower turns its great round face to follow the sun. Save the seeds for the wild birds, just as St. Francis recommended. If you live in one of our prairie states, you won't have to plant sunflowers; you will find them along every road and in every field. The sunflower is the state flower of Kansas.

A much smaller "sunflower" is the daisy, whose name really means "day's eye."

Each evening during Advent (or at least, on each Advent Sunday), write down the time of sunset. Are the days growing longer or shorter?

To mark off Christmas waiting, tape a cardboard Advent calendar to the window. Open one small translucent picture each day until Christmas Eve.

The Lord bless you and keep you;
The Lord make his face shine upon you!
 Blessing for the People, Numbers 6:24

REFERENCES, BIBLIOGRAPHY

Barth, Edna   *Holly, Reindeer, and Colored Lights* (New York: Seabury Press, 1971)

Bille-De Mot, Eleonore   *The Age of Akhenaten* (New York: McGraw Hill, 1966)

Brandon, S.G.F. (editor)   *Dictionary of Comparative Religion* (New York: Scribner's, 1970)

Daniel-Rops, Henri   *Daily Life in the Time of Jesus* (New York: Hawthorn, 1962)

Ellis, Peter F.   *The Men and Message of the Old Testament* (Collegeville, Minn.: Liturgical Press, 1963)

Epstein, Sam and Beryl   *Spring Holidays* (Champaign, Ill.: Garrard Pub. Co., 1964)

Guirand, Felix (editor)   *New Larousse Encyclopedia of Mythology* (translation; New York: Hamlyn Publishing, Prometheus Press, 1968 edition)

Hastings, James (editor)   *Encyclopedia of Religion and Ethics* (New York: Scribner's, 1934)

Ickis, Marguerite   *The Book of Religious Holidays and Celebrations* (New York: Dodd, Mead & Co., 1966)

Johnson, Lois S.   *Happy Birthdays Round the World* (New York: Rand McNally, 1963)

McKenzie, John L. *Dictionary of the Bible* (Milwaukee: Bruce, 1965)

McSpadden, Joseph W. *The Book of Holidays* (New York: Thomas Y. Crowell, 1958)

New Catholic Encyclopedia Catholic University of America (New York: McGraw Hill, 1967)

Purdy, Susan *Jewish Holidays* (Philadelphia: Lippincott, 1969)

Ricciotti, Giuseppe *Life of Christ* (trans. by Alba Zizzamia) Milwaukee: Bruce, 1952)

Seyffert, Oscar *Dictionary of Classical Antiquities* (edited by Nettleship and Sandys) (New York: Meridian, 1956)

Smaridge, Norah *Feast Days and Fun Days* (New York: Guild Press, 1966—paperback)

Spicer, Dorothy Gladys *46 Days of Christmas* (New York: Coward-McCann, 1960)

Weiser, Francis X. *The Christmas Book* (New York: Harcourt, Brace, 1952)

——— *Handbook of Christian Feasts and Customs* (New York: Paulist Press, 1963—paperback)

——— *The Year of the Lord in the Christian Home* (Collegeville, Minn.: Liturgical Press, 1964)

Wernecke, Herbert H. *Christmas Customs Around the World* (Philadelphia: Westminster Press, 1959)

ARTICLES

Mora, Bishop Bartholomew   "Constantine Made a Law" *The Way,*
    May, 1972

Klein, Charlotte   "Jewish Women in the Time of Mary of Nazareth"
    The Bible Today, April, 1972

130

77 02108 138